Papa Panov's
Special Day

This book is on loan from
Library Services for Schools

County Council

For Robin, Nicholas and Linda M.H.
To Linda J.D.

Text copyright © 1976 Mig Holder
Illustrations copyright © 2003 Julie Downing
This edition copyright © 2003 Lion Hudson

The moral rights of the author and illustrator
have been asserted

A Lion Children's Book
an imprint of
Lion Hudson plc
Mayfield House, 256 Banbury Road,
Oxford OX2 7DH, England
www.lionhudson.com
ISBN 0 7459 4564 3

First edition 1976
Second edition 1988
This edition 2003
3 5 7 9 10 8 6 4 2

A catalogue record for this book is available
from the British Library

Typeset in 14/21 BernhardMod BT
Printed and bound in Singapore

A CLASSIC FOLK TALE ADAPTED BY LEO TOLSTOY

Papa Panov's Special Day

RUBEN SAILLENS

Retold by MIG HOLDER

Illustrations by JULIE DOWNING

LION
Children's Books

A long time ago, almost too long ago to remember, there lived an old shoemaker. His home was far away, almost too far to imagine, in a small Russian village.

His name was Panov. But nobody called him Panov or Mister Panov or even shoemaker Panov; wherever he went in the village he was known as Papa Panov because everybody was so fond of him.

Papa Panov was not very rich – all he owned in the world was one small room looking out onto the village street. And in that one room he lived and slept and made shoes.

But neither was he very poor. He had all his shoemaking tools, a beautiful cast-iron stove to cook his food and warm his hands, a great wicker chair where he sat and snoozed, a good firm bed with a patchwork cover and a little oil lamp to see by when evening crept in.

And there were so many people who wanted new shoes made, or old ones patched and soled and heeled, that Papa Panov always had enough money to buy bread from the baker, coffee from the grocer and cabbage to make soup for his dinner.

So Papa Panov was quite happy – most of the time. Most of the time, his eyes would sparkle through his little round spectacles and he would sing and whistle and shout a cheery greeting to people passing by.

But today it was different. Papa Panov stood sadly in the window of his little shop and thought of his wife who had died many years before and of his sons and daughters who had all grown up and gone away. It was Christmas Eve and everybody else was at home with their families. Papa Panov looked up and down the village street and saw windows bright with candles and lamps and Christmas trees. He heard laughter and squeals of children playing games. And the faint smell of roasting meat crept through the cracks round the door and window of his little shop.

'Dearie, dearie,' said Papa Panov, pulling at his long white moustache and shaking his head slowly from side to side.

'Dearie, dearie,' and there was nobody to bring back the sparkle behind his little round spectacles.

Papa Panov sighed a great sigh. Then he slowly lit the oil lamp, went to a high shelf and lifted down an old brown book.

He dusted some scraps of leather off the bench, set a pot of coffee on the stove, sat down in the great wicker chair and began to read. Now Papa Panov had never been to school and could not read very well so, as he read, he ran his finger along the lines, saying the words out loud.

This was the story of Christmas. He read how a little boy, Jesus, was born, not in a good warm house but in a cowshed because there wasn't any room at the inn where his mother and father had asked to stay the night.

'Dearie, dearie,' said Papa Panov, pulling at his long moustache. 'If they had come here, they could have slept on my good bed and I would have covered the little boy with my patchwork quilt. I should like some company and a little child to play with.'

Papa Panov got up and poked the stove. It was becoming quite foggy outside so he turned up the lamp. He poured himself a mug of coffee and went back to his book.

He read how the wise men travelled across the desert to bring wonderful presents for the little boy Jesus – presents of gold and sweet-smelling spices.

'Dearie, dearie,' sighed Papa Panov. 'If Jesus came here, I shouldn't have anything to give him.'

Then he smiled and his eyes sparkled behind his little round spectacles. He got up from the table and went over to the high shelf. On it was a dusty box tied with string. He opened the box and unwrapped a pair of tiny shoes. Papa Panov held one small shoe in each hand and stood very still. They were the best shoes he had ever made.

He put them lovingly away in their box and lowered his old limbs back into the great wicker chair.

'That's what I would have given him,' he murmured.

He sighed a deep sigh and turned his attention to the book once more.

Now whether it was the warmth of the room or whether it was because it was getting late, who can say, but it wasn't long before Papa Panov's bony finger slid from the page, his little round spectacles slipped from his nose and he fell sound asleep.

Outside, the fog grew thicker. Dim figures glided past the window. But the old shoemaker slumbered on, snoring gently.

Suddenly, 'Papa, Papa Panov!' said a voice in the room. The old man jumped. His white moustache quivered. 'Who is it?' he cried, looking about him vaguely. He could see so little without his spectacles, but there seemed to be no one there.

'Papa Panov,' said the voice again. 'You wished that you had seen me, that I had come to your little shop and that you could bring me a gift. Look out into the street from dawn to dusk tomorrow and I will come. Be sure you recognize me for I shall not say who I am.'

Then all was quiet.

Papa Panov rubbed his eyes and sat up with a start. The charcoal in the stove had burned low and the lamp had gone out altogether, but outside, bells were ringing everywhere. Christmas had come.

'It was him,' said the old man to himself. 'That was Jesus.' He pulled at his moustache thoughtfully. 'Perhaps it was a dream – no matter, I will watch and hope that he will visit me on Christmas Day. But how shall I know him? He was not always a little boy; he grew to be a man, a king; they said he was God himself.'

The old man shook his head. 'Dearie, dearie,' he said slowly. 'I shall have to look very carefully.'

Papa Panov did not go to bed that night. He sat in his wicker chair, facing the window, and kept watch for the very first person to pass that way. Little by little the sun's rays crept up over the hill and began to brighten the long cobbled street outside.

Nobody was coming yet.

'I'll just make a nice pot of coffee for my Christmas breakfast,' said Papa Panov to himself cheerfully. 'I'll stoke up the charcoal in the stove and brew a huge jug of steaming coffee, but I'll keep an eye on the window all the while. I hope he will come today.'

So Papa Panov waited.

At last there was someone: a figure came into view at the far end of the winding road. Papa Panov pressed his face to the frosty glass. He was very excited — perhaps this was Jesus coming to see him. Then he stepped back, disappointed. The figure was coming closer, trudging slowly up the street, stopping every now and then. Papa Panov knew who it was — the roadsweeper who came each week with his barrow and broom.

Papa Panov felt cross. He had better things to do than watch
out for a roadsweeper. He was waiting for God, for the king,
Jesus. He turned away from the window impatiently and waited
till he thought the old fellow had passed by. But when he turned
back, the roadsweeper was there on the other side of the road
opposite Papa Panov's shop. He had set down his barrow and was
rubbing his hands together and stamping his feet. Papa Panov
felt sorry. The poor roadsweeper *did* look very cold. And imagine
having to work on Christmas Day!

Papa Panov tapped on the window but the old fellow did not
hear. So he went and opened the door of the little shop.

'Hey!' he called from the doorway. 'Hey old chap!' The roadsweeper looked round anxiously – people were often very rude to him because of his job – but Papa Panov was smiling.

'How about a cup of coffee?' he called. 'You look frozen to the bone.' The roadsweeper left his barrow at once.

'Don't mind if I do,' he said, shuffling into the tiny shop. 'It's very kind of you, very kind.'

Papa Panov poured out a mug of coffee from the jug on the stove.

'It's the least I can do,' he said, over his shoulder. 'After all it *is* Christmas.'

The old fellow sniffed. 'Well, this is all the Christmas I'll get.' As he warmed himself at the stove, thin drifts of steam rose from his damp clothes making a sour smell in the room.

Papa Panov returned to his place at the window and gazed up and down the street.

'You expecting visitors?' asked the roadsweeper gruffly. 'Not in the way, am I?'

Papa Panov shook his head, 'I… Well, have you heard of Jesus?' he asked.

'The Son of God?' asked the man.

'He's coming today,' replied Papa Panov.

The man looked at him in astonishment.

So Papa Panov told him the whole story.

'So that's why I'm watching out for him,' he finished at last.

The roadsweeper set down his mug, shook his head gloomily and made for the door. 'Well, the best of luck,' he said, 'and thanks for the coffee.' For the first time, the roadsweeper smiled. Then he hurried off into the street, collecting his barrow as he went.

Papa Panov stood in the open doorway and watched the roadsweeper disappear.

He looked up and down the street. The winter sun was shining brightly and its rays even gave off a little warmth, which was melting the frost on the window and the slippery ice on the cobblestones.

People were beginning to stir; a few drunks staggered home after the parties of the night before. Families in smart clothes hurried on their way to visit relatives. They nodded and smiled

at Papa Panov as they passed by. 'Merry Christmas, Papa Panov!'
they called. And the old shoemaker nodded and smiled back but
he did not stop them... he knew them all by name. He was
waiting for someone else.

He was just about to shut the door and go inside when
something caught his eye. Stumbling along in the shadows
close to the wall was a young woman carrying a baby. She
was very thin, her face was tired and her clothes were shabby.

Papa Panov watched her. Suddenly he called out, 'Hello, why don't you come in and warm yourself?' She looked up startled and made as if to run away. But she saw the old shoemaker's eyes sparkling behind his spectacles.

'You're very kind,' she said, as he stood aside for her to enter his little shop. Papa Panov shrugged.

'No, not really,' he said, 'you just looked so cold. Have you got far to go?'

'To the next village,' she replied flatly. 'About four miles. I used to lodge down at the mill but I have no money left to pay the rent. So I must go and ask my cousin to take me in. I have no husband, you see.'

The woman went inside and stood by the stove. Papa Panov took the baby in his arms. 'Will you share some bread and soup with me?' he asked. But the woman shook her head proudly.

'Well, some milk for the child then,' he said. 'I'll heat some on the stove. Don't worry' – his eyes sparkled – 'I've had children of my own!' The child chuckled and kicked his feet.

'Dearie, dearie,' said Papa Panov, shaking his head. 'The poor mite has no shoes.'

'I've none to give him,' said the young woman bitterly.

As Papa Panov sat feeding the little boy, a thought came into his mind. He pushed it away – but it came back. The box from his high shelf! The pair of tiny shoes he had made so long ago – they might fit the baby.

So Papa Panov got them down from the shelf and tried them on the child's feet. They fitted exactly. Perfect!

'There – you can have these,' he said softly. The young woman was overjoyed. 'How can I thank you enough?' she cried.

But Papa Panov didn't hear. He was looking anxiously out of the window. Had Jesus gone by while he was feeding the child?

'Something the matter?' asked the young woman kindly.

'Have you heard of Jesus who was born at Christmas?' replied the old shoemaker.

The girl nodded.

'He's coming today,' said Papa Panov. 'He promised.' And he told her all about the dream – if it was a dream.

The young woman listened until he had finished. She looked as if she didn't believe him at all, but she patted the old shoemaker's hand kindly.

'Well, I hope your dream comes true,' she said. 'You deserve it, for being so good to me and the baby.'

And with that she went on her way.

Papa Panov closed the door behind her and, after boiling up a big dish of cabbage soup for his dinner, took his place at the window once again.

Hours ticked by and people came and went. Papa Panov looked closely at everyone who passed. But Jesus did not come.

Then he began to be afraid. Perhaps Jesus had come and he had not recognized him. Perhaps he had passed by quickly when Papa Panov had turned away just for a second to poke the fire

or boil the soup! The old shoemaker could sit still no longer.
He went to the door of the little shop for one last look.

All sorts of people came by: children and old men, beggars
and grannies, cheerful people and grumpy people; to some he
gave a smile, to some a nod and to the beggars a coin or a hunk
of bread.

But Jesus did not come.

As dusk fell and the grey December fog began creeping up again, the old shoemaker sadly lit his oil lamp and sat down wearily in the great wicker chair. He took out his book to read, but his heart was too heavy and his eyes were too tired to make out the words on the page.

'It was only a dream after all,' he said to himself sadly. 'I wanted to believe it so much; I wanted him to come.'

And two great tears welled up behind his spectacles and filled his eyes, so that he could hardly see.

At once it seemed as if there was someone in the room. Through his tears Papa Panov seemed to see a long line of people passing across the little shop. The roadsweeper was there and the woman and her child – all the people he had seen and spoken to that day.

And as they passed they whispered, one by one, 'Didn't you see me? Didn't you see me, Papa Panov?'

'Who are you?' cried the old shoemaker, struggling out of his chair. 'Who are you? Tell me!'

And there came the same voice as the night before, though where it came from, Papa Panov could not have said.

'I was hungry and you gave me food, I was thirsty and you gave me water, I was cold and you took me in. These people you have helped today – all the time you were helping them, you were helping me!'

Then everything was quiet.

The tears dried in the old man's eyes and there was no one to be seen.

'Dearie, dearie,' said Papa Panov slowly, pulling at his long white moustache. 'So he came after all. I'll remember that whenever I read the Christmas story.'

The old shoemaker shook his head from side to side thoughtfully. Then he smiled and the sparkle came back behind his little round spectacles.

Other picture stories from Lion Children's Books